Holy Places

The Ganges

and Other Hindu Holy Places

Victoria Parker

Raintree

For information, address the publisher:
Raintree, 100 N. LaSalle, Suite 1200, Chicago, IL 60602

Design by Joanna Sapwell and StoryBooks
Printed and bound in China.

07 06 05 04 03
10 9 8 7 6 5 4 3 2 1

Library of Congress Cataloging-in-Publication Data

Parker, Victoria.
    The Ganges / Victoria Parker.
      p. cm. -- (Holy places)
    Summary: An introduction to Hinduism which focuses on some
  holy sites of the religion.
    Includes bibliographical references and index.
    ISBN 0-7398-6078-X (HC), 1-4109-0051-7 (Pbk.)
    1. Hinduism--Juvenile literature. 2. Ganges River Delta (India
  and Bangladesh)--Juvenile literature. 3. Civilization, Hindu
  --Juvenile literature.   [1. Hinduism. 2. Ganges River (India and
  Bangladesh)]   I. Title. II. Series.
    BL1203.P37 2003
    294.5′35′09541--dc21

2002014392

Acknowledgments
The Publishers would like to thank the following for permission to reproduce photographs: Associated Press pp. 14, 22; Christine Osborne Pictures pp. 5, 15, 17, 18, 20; Circa Photo Library pp. 13, 16; Circa Photo Library/John Smith p. 11; Corbis p. 28; Images Of India Picture Agency pp. 7, 10, 19; Link Picture Library p.24; Trip/B Vikander p. 25; Trip/F Good pp. 21, 26; Trip/H Rogers pp. 8, 9, 12, 23, 27, 29.

Co.. . . . . permission of Christine Osborne Pictures.

Every effort has been made to contact copyright holders of any material reproduced in this book. Any omissions will be rectified in subsequent printings if notice is given to the Publisher.

Contents

Words printed in bold letters, **like this**, are explained in the Glossary on page 30.

What Is the Ganges?

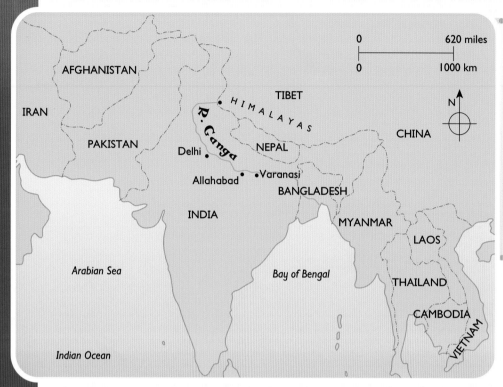

This map shows the Ganges River running through north India.

India has several mighty rivers. One is the ancient Ganges River, or Ganga. India is a huge land. In some parts it is a hot, dusty desert, and in others there are lush green plains. In the north lie the snowy mountains of the Himalayas and in the south there are sandy beaches and ocean.

The Ganges begins almost 1,312 feet (4,000 meters) high in the Himalayas. It flows from a **glacier** at a place called Gangotri. It flows down from there across the northern plains, through villages, towns, and cities. After a journey of 1,559 miles (2,510 kilometers), the river finally reaches the coast and drains into the Indian Ocean at the Bay of Bengal.

Other faiths

Not all people who live in India are Hindus. There are several other religions. Two other important religions in India are Islam and **Sikhism.** Hindus and Sikhs share some of their holy places and festivals. There are also **Buddhists, Jains,** and **Christians.**

Many of the people who live in India are Hindus. They follow a **religion** called Hinduism. There are seven great rivers in India that Hindus believe are **holy.** The holiest river of all is the Ganges. Every human, animal, and plant on Earth needs water to live. Many people in India believe that a mighty river, which brings so much life wherever it flows, is a **symbol** of the power of God, who gives life to all things.

The Ganges River flows from an ice field high up in the Himalayas.

5

Who Are the Hindus?

The first great **civilization** in India grew up around the Indus River about five thousand years ago. Fifteen hundred years later, people called **Aryans** arrived to live there. Over the next thousand years, each group's beliefs gradually mixed together to form the Hindu **religion.**

Most Hindus believe in a supreme spirit, whom they call Brahman, and who is neither male nor female. They believe that everything is created by Brahman, and Brahman is in everything.

The spirit inside a person is his or her **soul.** Hindus believe that when a person dies, the soul moves on to a new life as another person, or even as an animal or plant. Being born again is called reincarnation. Through reincarnation, a soul lives many different lives.

All Hindus want to break free from the endless cycle of death and rebirth so their soul can return to Brahman. Hindus say that this return to Brahman is a state of perfect happiness called **moksha.**

Because Hindus believe that a person's soul can be reborn as an animal, they treat all creatures kindly. Many Hindus do not eat meat.

Holy cows

Hindus have special respect for cows. They believe it is wrong to harm or kill a cow—even by accident. A person's soul is often pictured as a white cow. Cows are also givers of milk, and so they are a **symbol** of the source of life itself. Others think cows are special because in ancient times they were a form of wealth.

In India, cows are allowed to wander wherever they like.

The Ganges Legend

Hindus honor the Ganges River as a goddess called Ganga. They believe that the Ganges is Ganga's home on Earth. They believe that in ancient times the Ganges did not flow on Earth. It began from the god Vishnu's toe and flowed through heaven. A story tells how the Ganges came down to Earth.

A king called Sagar once lost a precious horse and sent his sons to search for it. The princes accused a **holy** man of stealing it. The holy man was so angry that he wished them dead. The princes were burned to ashes on the spot.

This painting shows the goddess Ganga pouring water onto Earth.

Gods and goddesses

Hindus believe that Brahman is so great that it is impossible to understand. Instead, they worship Brahman through many gods and goddesses. Each god or goddess represents a different power or aspect of Brahman.

The holy man announced that the princes' **souls** could only reach **moksha** if Ganga washed over the land. Neither King Sagar's grandson nor his son, Dilip, could bring Ganga down from heaven. Finally, Dilip's son, Bhagirath, offered many prayers that pleased Ganga and she began to flow toward Earth.

The rushing river was so mighty that she would have smashed the Earth to pieces, but the great god Shiva caught Ganga in his hair. He let her trickle down gently into the Himalayas. Bhagirath led Ganga to the sea to look for the remains of the princes. As the holy waters washed over the ashes, the princes' souls were saved.

Many Hindu holy men live in lonely places to be on their own.

Why Is Varanasi a Holy City?

These Hindus are bathing in the Ganges at Varanasi.

The **holiest** place on the Ganges River is a city called Varanasi, also known as Benares. Hindus believe that the great god Shiva chose this city as his home on Earth. It has been a center for Hindu teaching for thousands of years.

Many Hindus believe that Varanasi is the most **sacred** place to bathe in the waters of the Ganges. All Hindus try to go to Varanasi at least once in their lifetime, even if it means traveling thousands of miles to get there. Millions of Hindus visit the city every year. They go down broad steps called **ghats** to bathe in the holy river. Then, they pray and worship at one of the many huge **temples** in the city.

DID YOU KNOW?

Another name for the city of Varanasi is Kashi. Kashi means "to shine," so some people call Varanasi the city of light. Hindus believe that Varanasi is such a holy place, it is as if Brahman is shining brightly there, lighting up the way for souls to be saved.

Hindus also believe that Varanasi is the best place in which to die. When a Hindu dies, his or her body is cremated, or burned. In Varanasi, Hindu cremations happen at Manikamika ghat, which is also called the burning ghat. Hindus ask to be cremated here and to have their ashes scattered into the Ganges. They believe that if they do this their **souls** will be nearer to breaking out of the cycle of death and rebirth. Many Hindus who die in other places ask their relatives to bring their ashes to Varanasi to scatter them on the Ganges.

These cremations are taking place on Manikamika ghat.

11

Shiva and the Gods

The great god Shiva, who helped to bring the Ganges down to Earth, is one of three main Hindu gods. Brahma is the creator god, who makes everything in the universe. Vishnu is the protector god, who helps to keep a balance between good and evil. Shiva is the destroyer god, who breaks things down so that new things can be created.

Shiva's wife is a very important goddess. She is worshiped in different forms. As Parvati, she is gentle and kind. As Durga, she is a warrior who rides a lion and fights demons. As Kali, she is fierce and bloodthirsty, and helps people to overcome their fears.

This painting shows Ganisha, the elephant-headed god of wisdom.

There are hundreds of other gods and goddesses who represent Brahman. Every Hindu has his or her own personal favorite to worship most of the time. Most Hindus have a **shrine** at their home, with a picture or image of their favorite god in it. This **sacred** image of the god is called a **murti**.

This is a murti of Shiva dancing.

What Happens in a Mandir?

Hindus worship at **temples** or mandirs. Each mandir is **dedicated** to a god, goddess, or **holy** man. Each Hindu mandir has a priest to look after it.

When worshipers arrive, they take off their shoes, ring a bell, and go inside to perform **puja.** Puja is a ceremony where Hindus show their love and respect for a god or goddess. The ceremony includes prayers and offerings to the god or goddess. The offering is usually some type of food. Any food that the worshiper offers is given back to them by the priest, with the god's blessing.

These Hindus are worshiping at a mandir at Varanasi.

There are big temples to important gods in many places along the Ganges River. In the ancient town of Haridwar, all the temples honor the goddess Ganga every night. Each temple holds an arti ceremony to Ganga at the same time. Afterwards, crowds of Hindus head to the river banks to make offerings, and hundreds of tiny lamps and flowers are set floating down the holy river.

Sometimes the priest will lead the worshipers in an **arti** ceremony. This is when the priest lights five lamps in a steel tray and circles it in front of the **murti** while the worshipers **chant** a prayer. The priest sprinkles water over the worshipers to show that blessings from the god are coming down upon them. Then, the arti tray is carried among the worshipers, to bring the blessing of the temple god to them.

This is the town of Haridwar on the Ganges River.

Hindu Worship at Home

This Hindu girl is worshiping before a shrine in her home.

Hindus believe there are many different ways to worship. One is at home, making offerings of **puja** to a **murti** in a household **shrine.** There is no special day or time when Hindus are meant to perform puja. Most Hindus like to make offerings every morning and evening.

A Hindu family makes a shrine by putting a murti on a table or shelf and decorating it with flowers, perfume, and candles. If the family has a bottle of holy water from the Ganges River, they might put this before the murti, too. There may also be pictures of other gods and goddesses, as well as the family's favorite.

DID YOU KNOW?

Murtis of Shiva often show him dancing. Hindus believe that Shiva's energy keeps the universe changing and moving. Sometimes shrines to Shiva contain a carved stone column instead of a murti. This is called a **lingam.** It is Shiva's special **symbol.** There are a great number of lingams at Varanasi.

To perform puja, Hindus take off their shoes and stand or sit cross-legged before the murti. They set down little gifts of flowers or food as offerings. Then, they concentrate by saying a verse of **holy** writing over and over again. This is called a **mantra.**

Often during puja, the mother of the family will look after the murti by carefully washing and drying it. Sometimes she will hang a garland of flowers on it or wrap a robe around it. Hindus believe that by showing respect for the image of the god, they are showing respect for Brahman.

This mother is caring for a household murti.

17

Pilgrimages to the Ganges

Hindus believe that if they do good deeds in this life, their next life will be closer to **moksha.** If they behave badly in this life, they will be reborn further away from moksha, perhaps as an animal. This idea is called **karma.** Hindus believe it is good karma if they make a journey to a **holy** place to worship there. This type of trip is called a **pilgrimage.**

There are many holy places along the Ganges besides Varanasi. Four places are especially important. Gangotri is the **glacier** high in the Himalayas where the Ganges begins. Haridwar is where the Ganges flows down to the plains. Allahabad (also known as Prayag) is where the Ganges joins another holy river, the Yamuna. Sagara Island is where the Ganges flows into the sea.

Pilgrims bathe at the source of the Ganges River.

Tirthas

Hindus believe that in holy places such as Varanasi, Ayodhya, and Mathura (all lie along the Ganges) a person can break free from Earth's cycle of death and rebirth and reach moksha. Such places are known as tirthas, which means crossing places. Hindus believe that it is easier to cross from this life into moksha at these places.

Once every 12 years, when the stars are in a special position in the sky, many Hindus make a pilgrimage to Allahabad. An enormous camp of tents springs up. Many pilgrims stay for a whole month to bathe in the waters and make offerings. This bathing fair is called Kumbh Mela. Over 10 million people attended the Kumbh Mela in 2001!

These Hindus are taking part in the Kumbh Mela at Allahabad.

19

Hindu Holy Books

These children are praying with their grandmother at home.

Hindus do not use the word Hinduism to describe their **religion.** They say that they follow Sanatan Dharma, which means "eternal truths." To Hindus, Sanatan Dharma is not just a religion but a way of life.

The first Hindu teachings are over 3,000 years old. They are known as the Vedas. Hindus believe they came from Brahman, the Supreme Spirit. The Vedas are beautiful poetry. They praise the gods of nature, such as the Sun, wind, and fire.

About 2,500 years ago, wise men began to teach pupils about the Supreme Spirit and the **soul** in all things. Their teachings are now called the Upanishads.

Many Hindu festivals celebrate the *Ramayana* poem. Hindus act out parts of the story in bright costumes with music and dancing. This way they remember the lessons about good and evil that lie behind the tale. Prince Rama's birthday is celebrated in a festival called Ramnavami. Hindus visit **temples** to see an image of baby Rama in a cradle and to hear readings from the *Ramayana*.

Many ordinary people found it difficult to understand the Upanishads. To make it easier, the wise men made their teachings into stories about gods and goddesses. One **sacred** story called the *Mahabharata* is the longest poem in the world. Another long poem called the *Ramayana* tells many exciting tales about a prince called Rama. Rama was the great god Vishnu in a human form.

Here are **ghats** and a temple in the town of Ayodhga on the Ganges River.

A Ganges Festival

This effigy of Durga is being lowered into the Ganges during the Dussehra festival.

Hindus celebrate a festival called Navaratri, also known as Dussehra. Many believe this is the most important festival of all.

At Navaratri, Hindus worship Shiva's wife in the form of the goddess Durga. Durga is a fierce protector of good and destroyer of evil. Hindu **holy** books say she is the daughter of the Himalaya mountains.

Hindus believe that each autumn, Durga comes to Earth for ten days to visit her family. Hindus show this by making an **effigy** of the goddess especially for the festival. Each evening for nine days there is a special **arti** ceremony followed by a meal and dancing.

At Dussehra ("the tenth day"), when Durga goes away, women kiss the effigy of the goddess goodbye. It is then lowered into the Ganges, where it sinks into the holy waters.

At Dussehra, Hindus also celebrate how Prince Rama won a battle with the demon Ravana. Ravana had stolen Rama's wife and taken her to his kingdom. Effigies of Ravana are burned on bonfires and the battle is acted out in plays called *Ramleelas*. In Delhi, the capital of India, there is an enormous fireworks display.

These children are celebrating the festival of Holi.

Other Hindu Holy Places

India is a very large country. There are hundreds of Hindu **holy** places spread across it. It can be difficult to reach many of them. People travel by planes, trains, and buses, but there are many poor people who travel on carts or on foot. However, Hindus believe that the more effort they make to go on a **pilgrimage,** the more they improve their **karma** and move closer to **moksha.**

Some Hindus gather water from the Ganges River at Varanasi and then walk to the south of India to a famous **temple** at Rameshwar to offer the water to the god Shiva. This is a journey of 2,400 miles (3,840 kilometers)!

This is the festival of Rath Yatra in the town of Puri.

Puri

Pilgrims travel to the east coast to Puri to worship Vishnu. At the Rath Yatra festival in June or July, an enormous chariot containing an **effigy** of Vishnu is dragged through the streets. Over 4,000 worshipers help to pull it along.

Pilgrims try to show great respect at holy places. Many pilgrims will give up certain foods as a sign of respect to the gods.

In the north of India is an ancient pilgrimage site called Badrinath. Worshipers of the god Vishnu climb a mountain to reach it. The weather can make the climb so dangerous that the temple is only open for six months of the year. On the west coast of India at Dwarka, there is a mighty temple to Krishna, one of the best-loved gods.

Some pilgrims bring home beads or charms for good luck.

Hindu Family Ceremonies

Hindu priests work out special dates by looking at the position of the stars and making charts called horoscopes. Priests draw up horoscopes for newborn babies to tell what their lives will be like. This is done at the baby's naming ceremony, about 10 days after its birth.

Hindus take part in several other family ceremonies during their lifetimes. These are called samskaras. One samskara is for boys about eight years old. The boy sits with his father and a priest around a **sacred** fire. They say prayers and then the priest loops a thread of strong cotton around the boy's shoulder. This marks the beginning of adulthood. The boy is meant to wear the thread for the rest of his life.

This Hindu boy is taking part in a sacred thread ceremony.

A Hindu wedding can be a huge celebration, lasting for several days, with hundreds of people invited to the wedding feast. The bride and groom are often chosen for each other by their parents. A Hindu bride usually wears a red dress called a sari and beautiful gold jewelry. They walk seven steps around a sacred fire, making a special promise to each other at each step. After the wedding, the bride goes to live with her husband's family.

This Hindu couple is getting married.

Mahatma Gandhi–A Hindu Holy Man

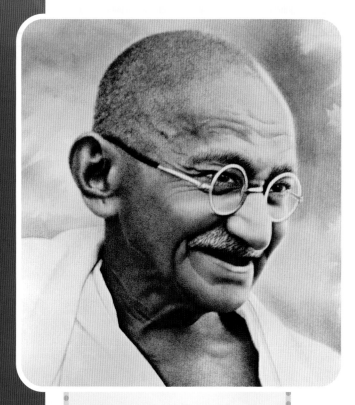

In January 1997, an important ceremony was held on the banks of the Ganges at Allahabad. Thousands of people watched and prayed as the final **urn of ashes** of a great Hindu leader was scattered into the **holy** river. This leader was a man named Mahatma Gandhi.

Mahatma Gandhi was killed in 1948 by a man who disagreed with his teachings.

Gandhi lived in India from 1869 to 1948 and grew up to be a lawyer. At that time, there was a lot of fighting in India between British soldiers, Hindus, and **Muslims.** Gandhi strongly felt that no one should use violence to get what they wanted. Instead, he led thousands of people in peaceful protests such as **sit-ins** and **hunger strikes.** He encouraged Indians of different **religions** to be friends.

Gandhi also worked hard to help poor people. Most Hindus believe that everyone is born into a different class of importance in society. The lowest people are given the dirtiest jobs. Other Hindus won't have anything to do with them. Gandhi thought this was wrong. He showed great kindness to these "untouchables" and worked hard to make their lives better. He called them Harijans, which means children of God.

This illustration from the *Bhagavad Gita* shows the god Krishna.

Gandhi and the Bible

Gandhi found strength and bravery in reading a Hindu holy book called the *Bhagavad Gita*. Its hero is the god of love, Krishna, who teaches people to do their duty and think of others before themselves. Gandhi's other favorite book was a part of the **Christian** Bible called the New Testament. This tells about the life of Jesus, who taught that it was important to help poor people, just as Gandhi himself believed.

Glossary

arti   main ceremony of worship at a Hindu temple

Aryans   race of people who lived in India in ancient times

Buddhists people who follow the teachings of the Buddha

chant   say something rhythmically over and over again

Christians   people who follow the spiritual teachings of a
man named Jesus, who lived about 2,000 years ago

civilization   society of people who live together in an
organized way, sharing laws and beliefs

dedicated   made important for just one person or thing

effigy   statue or model of a god

ghats   broad steps down to the edge of a holy river, where
Hindu cremations often take place

glacier   slowly moving field of ice, found high up on a mountain

holy (holiest)   blessed by or belonging to God. (Holiest is the
most holy.)

hunger strike   when people protest about something they
disagree with by refusing to eat anything

Jains people who follow a religion that began more than 2,500
years ago. The founder, Mahavira, taught a respect for life
and all living things.

karma   belief that the more good deeds you do in this life, the
more you will be rewarded in the next life

lingam   specially shaped piece of stone, a symbol for the god
Shiva

mantra   short prayer or saying that worshipers say over and
over again to help them concentrate on God

meditate to sit absolutely still and think very deeply on just one thing, trying to understand it better

moksha when a person's soul becomes free from living and dying and returns to Brahman

murti picture or statue of a god that is placed in a shrine

Muslim person who follows a religion called Islam, based on the teachings of a prophet called Muhammad (pbuh)

pilgrimage (pilgrims) journey someone makes to a holy place, especially to worship there. (Pilgrims are the people who do this.)

puja offerings Hindus make at a shrine when they worship

religion organized way of worshiping a god or gods

sacred something believed to be holy or special to a god or gods

shrine place of worship that is special for a certain holy person or thing

Sikhism religion that began in India over 500 years ago and grew from the teachings of a man called Guru Nanak

sit-in when people protest about something they disagree with by sitting down in an important place and refusing to move

soul part of a person that does not die when the body dies. Sometimes called the spirit.

symbol something that stands for something else

temple building where people worship a god or gods

urn of ashes ashes of a person's burned remains after cremation kept in a sealed jar called an urn

Index